Which Inventions Changed the World?

THIS EDITION
Editorial Management by Oriel Square
Produced for DK by WonderLab Group LLC
Jennifer Emmett, Erica Green, Kate Hale, *Founders*

Editors Grace Hill Smith, Libby Romero, Maya Myers, Michaela Weglinski;
Photography Editors Kelley Miller, Annette Kiesow, Nicole DiMella; **Managing Editor** Rachel Houghton;
Designers Project Design Company; **Researcher** Michelle Harris; **Copy Editor** Lori Merritt;
Indexer Connie Binder; **Proofreader** Larry Shea; **Reading Specialist** Dr. Jennifer Albro;
Curriculum Specialist Elaine Larson

Published in the United States by DK Publishing
1745 Broadway, 20th Floor, New York, NY 10019

Copyright © 2023 Dorling Kindersley Limited
DK, a Division of Penguin Random House LLC
24 25 26 10 9 8 7 6 5 4 3 2
003-334118-Sept/2023

A catalog record for this book
is available from the Library of Congress.
HC ISBN: 978-0-7440-7549-6
PB ISBN: 978-0-7440-7551-9

DK books are available at special discounts when purchased in bulk for sales promotions, premiums,
fundraising, or educational use. For details, contact: DK Publishing Special Markets,
1745 Broadway, 20th Floor, New York, NY 10019
SpecialSales@dk.com

Printed and bound in China

The publisher would like to thank the following for their kind permission to reproduce their images:
a=above; c=center; b=below; l=left; r=right; t=top; b/g=background

Alamy Stock Photo: Dpa Picture Alliance / Karl-Josef Hildenbrand 17b; **Depositphotos Inc:** Narin_Photo 28-29;
Dorling Kindersley: Dave King / Science Museum, London 19bl, Clive Streeter / The Science Museum, London 9t;
Dreamstime.com: Absente 22t, Albertshakirov 8cra, Andrey Armyagov / Cookelma 6-7, Ken Backer 16b, Dashark 3cb, Dndavis 13cl,
Dobyter 12cra, Ciprian Florin Dumitrescu 11tr, HodagMedia 13br, Icefront 13ca, Krishtopaytis 24cl, Kaling Megu 14t,
Oksanaphoto 12cl, One Photo 7tl, Pojoslaw 4-5, Prostockstudio 1b, 14cla, 25b, 27bl, Konstantin Shaklein 11, Spaceheater 21t,
Lawrence W Stolte 24, James Vallee 10t, Stoyan Yotov 26t; **Fotolia:** Alperium 7bl; **Getty Images:** Drew Angerer / Staff 25tr,
Archive Photos / Harold M. Lambert 23t, Bettmann 22-23b; **Getty Images / iStock:** mbbirdy 18;
Shutterstock.com: Everett Collection 20b, Morphart Creation 15br, Regien Paassen 8b

Cover images: *Front:* **Depositphotos Inc:** tycoon b; **Dreamstime.com:** Dezzor, Valya567 ca; **Shutterstock.com:** Dmitry Natashin cb;
Back: **Dreamstime.com:** Dan Talson clb

All other images © Dorling Kindersley
For more information see: www.dkimages.com

For the curious
www.dk.com

Which Inventions Changed the World?

Libby Romero

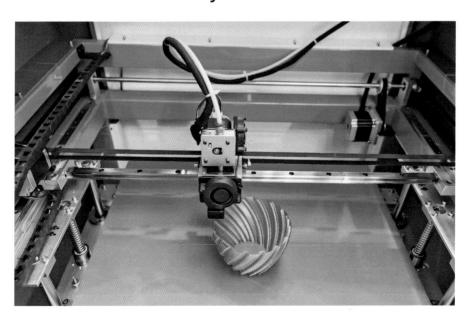

Contents

On the Move

Bigger! Better! Higher! Faster! People invent things for lots of reasons.

Inventions solve problems. Inventions can be fun. Some are so amazing that they change the world.

Think about this. Long ago, sailors used the Sun and the stars to navigate the seas. Then, the compass was invented. It pointed people in the right direction.

Finding Your Way

Many electronic devices have GPS. GPS links to satellites in space. It finds locations on Earth.

Today, Global Positioning System (GPS) shows people how to find places. Inventions have changed how people move around the world.

People like to travel. The wheel made it a lot easier for people to get around. But the first wheel wasn't used for transportation. It was used to make pottery!

Eventually, people put wheels on chariots and wagons.

The first bicycle was invented in 1817. It didn't have a chain, pedals, or brakes. Unlike a wagon, it didn't need a horse to make its wooden wheels move. It used people power! The bicycle was a cheap and easy way to travel.

Travel got even faster when people invented engines. First, there were steam engines. Steam engines could pull heavy trains down the tracks.

Then came gasoline-powered engines. They were a popular choice in automobiles.

Today, rocket engines take people into outer space.

Many travel inventions were inspired by nature. Lots of ideas came from birds. The idea for airplanes came from watching birds fly.

kingfisher

bullet train

The bullet train was designed to look like a kingfisher's bill. The shape makes the train quieter.

Now, scientists are studying how hummingbirds fly to build a better helicopter.

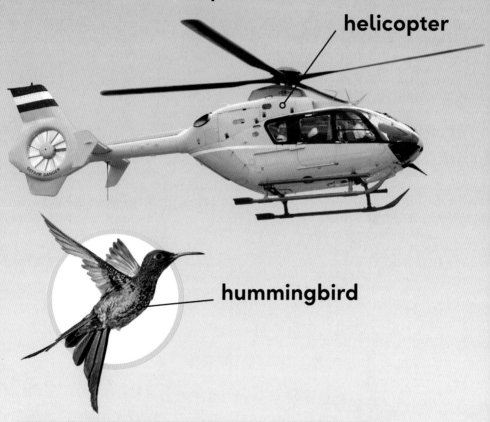

helicopter

hummingbird

The Wright Brothers

Orville and Wilbur Wright spent a lot of time studying birds. Then, they invented their flying machine. In 1903, Orville made the first powered flight in history.

Medical Marvels

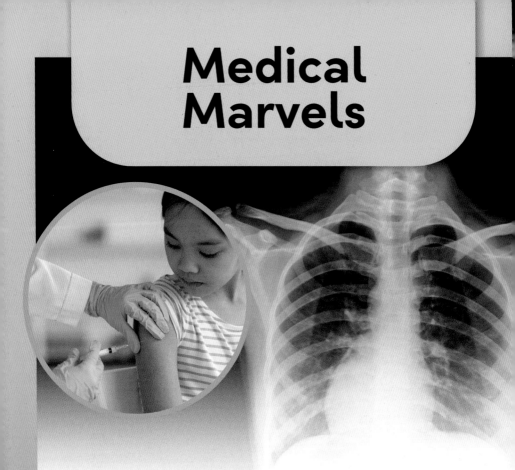

Staying healthy is important. Scientists have come up with some pretty amazing things that help us fight disease and infection.

These medical inventions help people live longer and better lives.

Penicillin was one of the first antibiotics. Antibiotics kill the bacteria that cause infections.

Vaccines protect you from certain diseases. They give your body what it needs to fight off illness.

X-rays allow doctors to see inside the human body—without cutting it open! They take a picture of the inside of your body.

Marie Curie

During World War I, Marie Curie invented a small, portable X-ray machine. She trained women to use it in the field.

Building the Future

Ancient people invented tools. They sharpened stones to cut things. They tied sticks together with rope to build things. They shaped metal to make nails. Nails made wooden structures stronger and more complex.

Concrete made buildings even stronger. With the invention of steel beams, buildings got taller.

Today, people can design a building on a computer. A huge 3D printer can make the walls, floors, and ceiling. Builders put the parts together.

Multiuse Printer

3D printers can make anything that people design on a computer: tools, bicycles, and even parts to replace human bones!

Another game changer was the electric light bulb. Light bulbs let people see inside buildings, at any time of day or night.

The light bulb sparked a new way of life. People stayed up later. Businesses stayed open later. People could safely gather after dark.

Thomas Edison

Many inventors created electric light bulbs. Thomas Edison made the first one that was reliable and long-lasting.

Creative Communication

One way to change the world is to change what people think. An invention that made that possible was the printing press with movable type.

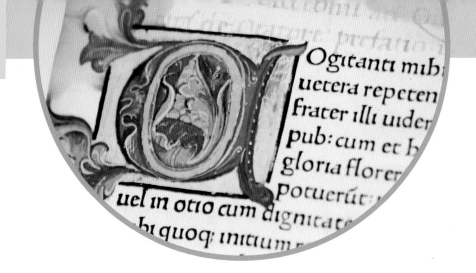

With this invention, printing was quicker and cheaper than ever before. For the first time, ordinary people could afford to buy books.

They read ideas from many different scholars. They started to question the ways things had always been done. They began to fight for change.

Other inventions helped new ideas spread fast. The telegraph was the first way to quickly send messages over a long distance.

Radio brought voices from around the world into people's homes.

TV let people see who was talking. It showed them what the world was like. It changed how people understood the world.

The telephone connected the world in a more personal way. A network of wires linked phones together. Now, people very far apart could talk to each other almost instantly.

Today, we have cell phones. They don't use wires. Messages travel on invisible radio waves through the air. People can talk, work, and play almost anywhere.

Few inventions have changed the world as much as computers. With the tap of a few keys, people have access to unlimited information. That information is stored on the internet. It is a worldwide system of computer networks.

Finding information is just a tiny part of what computers can do. People use computers to fly airplanes and control medical devices.

They use computers to operate power plants and the equipment inside them. There's even a tiny computer inside every mobile phone that allows you to talk with a friend.

Seeing Is Believing

Virtual reality (VR) is a fun way to use computers to play a game. It's also changing how people learn. Pilots, doctors, and astronauts all learn new skills using VR technology.

People come up with new inventions all the time. Usually, an invention is a better version of something that already exists.

But sometimes, it is brand-new—an idea that nobody ever thought of before.

Inventions can make life easier.
They can make life more fun.
They can change the world.
Are you ready?

Glossary

Antibiotic
A substance that prevents or stops infection by killing bacteria

Bacteria
One-celled organisms that can cause disease

Chariot
A two-wheeled, horse-drawn vehicle used in ancient times

Concrete
A solid building material made by mixing cement, sand, and gravel or broken rocks with water

Immune
Protected from a disease, either naturally or by a vaccine

Invent
To think of or create something new

Navigate
To plan or manage a way to get somewhere

Portable
Able to be moved or carried easily

Scholar
A person who has gained much knowledge from research and study

Steel
A hard, strong metal made from iron and carbon

Vaccine
A substance that is introduced to the body to prevent disease

Virtual reality
An experience created by a computer program that resembles the sights and sounds of the real world

Index

Quiz

Answer the questions to see what you have learned. Check your answers in the key below.

1. What are two inventions that have made it easier for people to navigate the world?

2. What inspired people to invent airplanes?

3. Which invention protects people from certain diseases?

4. Why was the telegraph an important invention?

5. Draw a picture of your favorite invention. How do you think it has changed the world?

1. The compass and GPS 2. Watching birds fly 3. Vaccines
4. It was the first way to quickly send messages over a long distance
5. Answers will vary